Toilet Train
Your Dog
In
Seven Days

Toilet Train Your Dog In Seven Days

Amanda Walker

Published by Amanda Walker, 2023.

TOILET TRAIN YOUR DOG IN SEVEN DAYS

First edition. April 9, 2023.

ISBN: 979-8224488056

Written by Amanda Walker.

Toilet training your furry friend is a vital part of being a responsible pet owner. Whether you are bringing home a new puppy or adopting an adult dog, proper house training is essential. This process not only teaches your dog important life skills but also strengthens the bond between you and your four-legged companion.

It is vital to remember that you are not only training a puppy or new dog, but you are also training yourself into making new habits and you will need to make the commitment to do so if you want your pet to be trained. Even when your tired and do not feel like it. Any break in the level of consistency required to teach your pet anything will just mean you have to start from scratch and it will take longer for them to learn, regardless of if you are teaching them house training or a new trick

It's essential to note that dogs don't develop full bladder control until they reach around 12 months of age. However, if you are training an adult dog that hasn't been house trained before, the process may take longer.

When you start toilet training, it's essential to provide your dog with plenty of opportunities to go outside. Actively supervising your furry friend and keeping a watchful eye on them is vital to the success of the training process. Make sure to offer plenty of opportunities to go to the toilet in the correct place, especially when they wake up, after every meal, after playtime, before bed, before you leave them alone, and upon your return. For young puppies, it's best to offer opportunities to go every 45 minutes.

Recognizing the signs that your dog needs to toilet is crucial to the training process. These signs can include fidgeting, sniffing around, and beginning to circle before squatting. When you notice these signs, quickly take your dog to the appropriate area and use a verbal cue such as "toilet" to associate it with the correct behaviour. When your furry friend finishes toileting, offer immediate rewards such as praise, treats, and playtime. Before going back inside, take a short walk or play with your dog to avoid them learning that toileting ends their time outside, leading them to hold on for longer.

If you notice your dog about to go in the wrong place, it's essential to interrupt them without punishing them, such as calling their name. Take them calmly to the correct spot and praise them when they use the correct area. Avoid shouting, as this can teach your dog that it's only safe to go when you're not around.

In conclusion, toilet training your dog is essential for both your furry friend's well-being and your relationship with them. By providing plenty of opportunities to go outside, recognizing the signs, and using positive reinforcement, you'll be on your way to a successful training journey.

7 Day Guide
Day 1 - Make a Feeding Schedule

Starting a new routine can be a daunting task, but when it comes to establishing a consistent potty routine for your furry friend, it's crucial to set up a plan from day one. On the first day, it's essential to establish a regular feeding schedule that you can easily stick with. A consistent feeding schedule not only helps your furry friend adjust to their new home, but it also sets the foundation for a consistent potty routine.

When deciding on your dog's feeding schedule, consider their age, breed, and weight, as well as any dietary restrictions or health concerns. A healthy diet is essential for a happy and healthy dog, so it's vital to choose high-quality food that meets their nutritional needs. A consistent feeding schedule with no food between meals is also key to establishing a regular potty routine. This helps your dog to develop a routine, making it easier for them to anticipate when it's time to go outside.

It's important to note that puppies have different nutritional needs than adult dogs, and their feeding schedule may differ. For instance, young puppies need to eat more frequently, so they may require smaller, more frequent meals throughout the day. As they grow older, you can gradually adjust their feeding schedule to meet their changing needs.

Once you've established a regular feeding schedule, make sure to provide your furry friend with plenty of fresh water throughout the day. Hydration is key to your dog's overall health and helps keep their digestive system functioning correctly.

Make sure to keep their water bowl clean and full, so they always have access to clean drinking water.

In conclusion, establishing a consistent feeding schedule is essential for setting up a regular potty routine for your furry friend. Take into account their nutritional needs, and choose high-quality food that meets their dietary requirements. A consistent feeding schedule with no food between meals helps your dog develop a routine, making it easier for them to anticipate when it's time to go outside. Providing plenty of fresh water is also crucial for their overall health and well-being. By establishing a solid routine from day one, you're setting your furry friend up for success in their new home.

Day 2 – Take Your Puppy Out CONSISTANTLY

One of the most important aspects of raising a puppy is establishing a consistent schedule for taking them outside to do their business. This not only helps to prevent accidents inside the house but also teaches the pup good behavior and potty training. On day 2 of having your new furry friend, it's essential to start implementing a routine that will work for both you and your pup.

First and foremost, it's crucial to take your puppy out first thing in the morning and just before you go to bed at night. This helps to ensure that they have a chance to relieve themselves before settling in for the night and upon waking up in the morning. For young puppies, it's also essential to take them outside every hour or so during the day. This includes after meals, when they wake up from naps, and ideally when they finish playing.

Puppies tend to have a higher frequency of eliminating waste than adult dogs, and it's normal for them to do so up to five times a day. Therefore, it's essential to be vigilant and take them outside frequently to avoid accidents inside the house. Additionally, taking them outside after playing or chewing on a toy or bone can help encourage them to do their business outside.

To instill good behavior, it's crucial to make the experience of going outside an enjoyable and rewarding one for your pup. After they do their business, offer them a treat and verbal praise to let them know that they did well. You can also take them on a short walk around the neighborhood as a reward for doing their business outside.

Remember that establishing a consistent schedule for taking your puppy outside is crucial for their potty training and overall behavior. By making it a positive experience, you can encourage good habits and help your pup feel comfortable and secure in their new home. With patience and persistence, you'll be well on your way to raising a well-trained and happy puppy.

Day 3 – Drive Consistency

Day three of having a new puppy is a critical time to teach them where they should relieve themselves. It's essential to establish a specific location where they can consistently go to the bathroom, as this will help them understand the routine and develop good habits. Repetition is key in potty training, and if you can teach your dog that one specific spot is the designated potty area, it will become second nature to them.

To begin, take note of where your puppy has done their business previously. Whether it's in the backyard or a nearby park, try to find an area that is easily accessible and convenient for both you and your dog. Once you've identified the spot, take your pup to that location every time you bring them outside to eliminate.

Be sure to use a consistent command or phrase when you take them to this spot, such as "go potty" or "do your business." Over time, your dog will learn to associate this command with the act of eliminating waste, and it will become easier to get them to go when you need them to.

It's also important to supervise your puppy during the potty training process. Keep an eye on them while they're outside to ensure they stay in the designated potty area and don't get distracted or wander off. If they start to sniff around or appear to be looking for a different spot, gently guide them back to the designated area and use your command to encourage them to go.

As with any training process, patience and consistency are essential. It may take some time for your puppy to fully understand where they are supposed to go, but with persistence and positive reinforcement, they will eventually develop good habits and be able to go to the bathroom on command. Remember to praise and reward your dog every time they go in the designated potty spot to encourage and reinforce the behaviour.

Day 4

On day four of having your new puppy, it's important to start paying attention to their behaviours and actions to spot the signs that they need to go potty. By being proactive and anticipating when your puppy needs to go, you can prevent accidents inside the house and further reinforce good potty training habits.

One of the most common signs that a dog needs to go potty is when they suddenly change their behaviour. This could include getting up from lying down and walking towards a different area of the house or yard. You may also notice your puppy whining, barking, circling, or sniffing around before they eliminate waste. If your puppy is unconfined, they may even scratch at the door to indicate that they need to go outside.

As you become more familiar with your puppy's body language and behaviour patterns, you'll be better equipped to anticipate their needs and prevent accidents. It's crucial to act quickly and bring them outside as soon as you notice any of these signals.

In addition to watching for physical signs, it's also important to establish a routine for taking your puppy outside. Stick to a consistent schedule for taking them out to eliminate, and make sure to take them out after meals, naps, and playtime. By establishing a routine, your puppy will begin to anticipate when it's time to go outside and will develop good potty training habits.

Remember to praise and reward your puppy every time they eliminate waste outside to reinforce good behaviour. Over time, with patience, consistency, and attention to their body language, your puppy will become fully potty trained and able to communicate their needs effectively

As you continue to work on spotting the signs that your puppy needs to go potty, it's important to remain patient and consistent. It may take some time for your puppy to fully understand what is expected of them and develop good habits.

One helpful tip is to keep a potty training journal to track your puppy's progress. Record when they go potty, how often they need to go, and any accidents that occur. This can help you identify patterns and adjust your training approach as needed.

In addition to paying attention to your puppy's behavior, you can also use tools to help with potty training. For example, you can use a bell or chime to signal to your puppy that it's time to go outside. By consistently ringing the bell before taking them out, your puppy will learn to associate the sound with going potty.

It's also important to be consistent in your discipline when accidents do occur. Avoid punishment, as this can confuse and scare your puppy. Instead, simply clean up the mess and move on. Remember, accidents are a normal part of the potty training process, and with patience and consistency, your puppy will eventually learn to go potty outside every time.

Finally, as you work on potty training your puppy, it's important to remember that every dog is different. Some puppies may catch on quickly and become fully trained in just a few weeks, while others may take several months to fully grasp the concept. Be patient, and don't give up hope. With the right approach, your puppy will eventually become fully potty trained and a happy, well-behaved member of your family.

Day 5 – Reinforcement

As you approach day five of potty training your puppy, you may start to notice that they are having fewer accidents inside the house. This is a good sign that your hard work is paying off! However, it's important to remember that accidents may still happen, especially if your puppy is under a year old.

It's crucial to approach accidents in the right way to avoid confusing or scaring your puppy. When you catch your puppy eliminating in the house, don't punish them. Instead, clap loudly to let them know that what they did was inappropriate. This will help to get their attention and make them stop what they are doing.

Next, immediately take your puppy outside by calling their name or gently leading them by the collar. It's important to take them outside right away so that they can finish eliminating outside where it's appropriate. Once they have finished going potty outside, be sure to respond with praise and/or a small treat to reinforce the good behaviour.

It's important to avoid cleaning up your puppy's accidents with an ammonia-based cleaner. This is because the smell of ammonia may actually attract your puppy back to the spot and prompt them to eliminate there again. Instead, use an enzymatic cleaner to minimize odours and clean up any messes thoroughly.

As you continue to work on potty training your puppy, it's important to remain patient and consistent. Remember that accidents are a normal part of the process, and it may take some time for your puppy to fully understand what is expected of them.

Day 6- Evaluation

Potty training a puppy is an essential part of responsible pet ownership. It not only makes your life easier but also contributes to your pet's well-being. By day six of your puppy's potty training, you should have seen some significant progress in your furry friend's ability to understand when and where to go potty.

Day six is an essential day for monitoring the consistency of your training efforts. By this point, you should have a routine in place, including feeding times, potty breaks, and playtime. Consistency is key when it comes to training a puppy, and day six is an excellent time to assess how well you and your puppy are maintaining this consistency.

However, despite your best efforts, your puppy may still be struggling with potty training, even at this stage. If your puppy is having accidents in the house consistently, it's essential to address this issue before it becomes a long-term problem.

One possible reason for your puppy's lack of progress could be an underlying medical condition. It's possible that your puppy is struggling with bladder or bowel control due to an illness or injury. In such cases, it's essential to take your puppy to the vet to rule out any medical conditions that may be causing the problem.

Common medical conditions that can impact your puppy's potty training progress include urinary tract infections, bladder stones, and diabetes. A urinary tract infection can cause your puppy to feel a constant need to urinate, while bladder stones can cause pain and difficulty urinating. Diabetes, on the other hand, can cause frequent urination, leading to accidents inside the house.

If you suspect that your puppy's lack of progress is due to a medical condition, it's crucial to get them checked out by a veterinarian as soon as possible. Early diagnosis and treatment can help prevent further complications and improve your puppy's quality of life.

It's important to remember that potty training is a process that takes time and patience. Not all puppies learn at the same pace, and it's essential to be consistent with your training efforts. If you're having trouble getting your puppy to understand where and when to go potty, consider seeking the help of a professional trainer or behaviourist. With patience, consistency, and a little bit of professional guidance, your puppy will be potty trained in no time!

Day 7 – Completion

Congratulations! You have successfully completed a full week of consistent house training for your puppy. By this point, your puppy should be showing significant progress in understanding where to go potty and should be able to communicate their need to eliminate.

It's important to continue the routine of regular feeding times and taking your puppy outside to the same location to reinforce their training. Consistency is key in ensuring your puppy's success in potty training, and reinforcing their good behavior with positive reinforcement will help decrease the chance of any setbacks.

As you continue with your puppy's training, it's important to pay attention to any areas where they may still be struggling. If your puppy is having trouble with one specific aspect of potty training, such as signaling when they need to go outside or holding their bladder for longer periods, it's essential to focus on that specific area and reinforce good behavior when they do get it right.

Positive reinforcement can be an effective way to encourage your puppy to continue their good behavior. This can include offering treats, praise, or playtime when your puppy goes potty outside or signals their need to eliminate. It's important to use positive reinforcement consistently and immediately after your puppy exhibits the desired behavior to reinforce the connection between their behavior and the positive reinforcement.

It's also essential to be patient and understanding as your puppy continues to learn. Potty training takes time, and not all puppies learn at the same pace. Your puppy may have accidents inside the house occasionally, and it's important to avoid scolding or punishing them for these accidents, as this can be counterproductive and harm their progress.

In conclusion, by the end of the first week of consistent house training, your puppy should be showing significant progress in understanding where and when to go potty. Continue with your regular feeding and potty break schedule, reinforce positive behavior with positive reinforcement, and focus on areas where your puppy may still be struggling. With patience and consistency, your puppy will become potty trained in no time!

Increase the Time Between Bathroom Breaks

After successfully establishing a routine around your puppy's bathroom breaks, it's time to start increasing the time between their outdoor visits. A general rule of thumb to determine how often your puppy needs to go outside is to consider their age. A good guideline is that a puppy can hold their bladder for about as many hours as they are months old, plus one. So, for instance, if your puppy is three months old, they should be able to "hold it" for up to four hours.

However, it's important to remember that your puppy will still need to go potty shortly after their meals and first thing in the morning, regardless of their age. Puppies have small bladders and may need to go outside more frequently than adult dogs, especially during the early stages of potty training.

As your puppy becomes more comfortable with their routine and demonstrates more control over their bladder, you can gradually increase the time between their outdoor visits. Keep in mind that every puppy is different and may have different needs, so it's important to observe your puppy's behavior and adjust their routine accordingly.

Additionally, if you plan on being away from home for an extended period, it's essential to make arrangements for someone to let your puppy out to go potty. Holding their bladder for too long can cause discomfort, and your puppy may have an accident in the house if they are unable to hold it.

In conclusion, while a good rule of thumb to determine how often your puppy needs to go outside is that they can hold their bladder for about as many hours as they are months old, plus one, it's important to remember that puppies still have small bladders and may need to go outside more frequently than adult dogs. As your puppy becomes more comfortable with their routine and demonstrates more control over their bladder, you can gradually increase the time between their outdoor visits. Remember to make arrangements for someone to let your puppy out if you plan on being away from home for an extended period.

House Training Your Puppy With a Crate

When it comes to potty training your puppy, using a crate can be a helpful tool, depending on your schedule and your dog's temperament. Crates can aid in keeping a better eye on your puppy and recognizing signals that they need to eliminate. Additionally, crates can teach your pup to hold it until you open the crate and bring them outside.

It's essential to use the right size crate for your puppy. It should be large enough to allow your puppy to stand, turn around, and lie down comfortably, but not too large that they could use a corner of the crate as an elimination spot. If your dog does start eliminating in the crate, it's best to stop using this method. They may have picked up this habit from a previous home, or they may be too young to handle the crate.

While using a crate, it's important to take your puppy outside regularly for bathroom breaks. If you need to use a crate for more than two hours at a time, make sure your dog has consistent access to fresh water. It's important to note that your puppy may eventually be able to stay in the crate and hold it for the length of an entire workday. However, during the first eight months to a year, someone should be around during the day to give them regular breaks from the crate.

Using a crate should never be used as a punishment or for extended periods. It's crucial to make the crate a positive experience for your puppy. A crate should be associated with comfort and safety, not punishment. Gradually increasing the amount of time your puppy spends in the crate can help them become more comfortable and less anxious. Additionally, providing your puppy with chew toys or treats while in the crate can help keep them occupied and make the experience more enjoyable.

In conclusion, using a crate can be a helpful tool for potty training your puppy, but it's essential to use the right size crate and ensure it's a positive experience for your puppy. Gradually increasing the amount of time your puppy spends in the crate and providing them with chew toys or treats can help them become more comfortable and less anxious. Remember to take your puppy outside regularly for bathroom breaks and never use a crate for punishment or extended periods.

House Training With Puppy Pads

If you're unable to bring your puppy outside frequently enough for him to learn that it's the only acceptable place to eliminate, then using puppy pads or paper training is a viable alternative. However, it's important to note that this method can potentially prolong the potty training process.

To train your puppy to use a puppy pad, begin by placing it in a designated area of the house and leading your puppy to it after meals or when he signals that he needs to eliminate. It's important to consistently use the same area and reinforce good behavior with praise and/or treats.

It's essential to note that using puppy pads should only be a temporary solution. The ultimate goal is for your puppy to eliminate exclusively outside. To transition your puppy from puppy pads to outside elimination, gradually move the pads closer to the door leading outside. Once your puppy is consistently using the pads at the door, begin taking him outside instead.

Keep in mind that while using puppy pads or paper training, accidents can still happen, and it's important to clean up any messes thoroughly and quickly to prevent your puppy from being attracted back to that spot.

Regardless of whether you choose to use puppy pads or not, it's crucial to remain consistent with your potty training methods. Set a routine and stick to it to reinforce good habits and prevent setbacks. With time and patience, your puppy will learn to eliminate in the appropriate place, whether it's outside or on a puppy pad

What To Do If There's An Accident

If your dog starts to go in the wrong place, gently interrupt them without punishing them, for example, by calling their name. Take them calmly to the correct spot and reward them when they go. Don't shout at them, or they may learn that it's only safe to go when you're not around.

If you find an accident, never punish your dog, as they will not understand the connection between the accident and the punishment. Instead, clean the area thoroughly with warm water and biological washing powder to remove the smell and reduce the chance of your dog using that spot again. Do NOT use ammonia based chemicals such as bleach. Urine contains ammonia and by using ammonia based cleaning products your dog will associate the spot with the place they are meant to go though their heightened sense of smell. If you're concerned about your dog's toileting habits, seek advice from your vet.

Your Dog Wee's and Poo's When Home Alone

If your dog is going for a wee or poo indoors when separated from you they could be finding it difficult to cope alone

This type of separation-related behaviour is very common and there are some tips to help you work out what your dog is feeling when they're left alone and what to do about it in the next chapter

Final Notes On Toilet Training

It is essential to understand that every dog is unique, and therefore the process of potty training may vary from pup to pup. While some dogs may learn good habits around eliminating in just a few days, others may take a few months to grasp the concept, especially if they have picked up bad habits in the past.

Hence, it is crucial to remain patient and persistent throughout the process. Do not get frustrated or give up quickly, as it can be a setback for your dog's training. With consistent effort and reinforcement, your pup will eventually develop good habits and manners around eliminating.

Remember that your dog's progress is not only dependent on their breed or age, but also on their individual temperament and previous experiences. Therefore, be prepared to adjust your approach and methods as necessary to meet the needs of your pup.

In the end, all the hard work and effort will be worth it when you have a well-trained dog that is able to eliminate in appropriate places and times. So, stay committed to the training process, remain positive, and keep your expectations realistic.

How to deal with Separation Anxiety

Identifying the root cause of separation-related behaviour (SRB) in dogs can be a challenging task for pet owners. It can be particularly challenging since research indicates that nearly half of dogs with SRB do not display any obvious signs of anxiety or distress when their owners are present. Therefore, understanding your dog's behaviour and identifying the triggers that cause them to become anxious or agitated when left alone can be a complex process. It is important to pay close attention to your dog's behaviour and look for any signs of restlessness, barking, howling, or destructive behaviour that may indicate they are experiencing anxiety or distress.

Here are some tips to deal with separation anxiety, however in extreme cases seeking the guidance of a veterinarian or a qualified animal behaviourist can also help you to understand the underlying causes of your dog's separation anxiety and develop effective strategies to manage their behaviour.

1. Leave a Special Treat or Toy

Leaving your dog alone can be a challenging experience for both you and your pet. To make it easier for your dog, it's important to make sure that they have stimulating activities to engage in while you're gone. One great way to keep your dog entertained is to give them a long-lasting chew or treat. A stuffed "kong" toy, a meat-flavored chew, or a treat ball are all great options.

It's important to introduce these items to your dog when you are present to ensure they are comfortable with them. If they show interest and excitement when you're home, it's a good sign that they will engage with them when you're not there. If, however, they show no interest in the items, this could indicate that your dog is experiencing anxiety when left alone. In this case, you may need to seek additional support to help your dog feel more comfortable when you're away.

It's also important to remember that treats should be taken out of your pet's daily food allowance to avoid overfeeding. Feeding your pet too many treats can lead to weight gain and other health problems. Providing your pet with stimulating activities while you're away can help alleviate boredom and anxiety, making it a more positive experience for both you and your furry friend.

2.Encourage your pet to relax during their alone time

To help your dog relax when you leave, it's a good idea to take them for a walk before you go out so they can go to the toilet and burn off some energy. Try to return home at least half an hour before you plan to leave to give your dog some time to settle down. Ensure that they're not hungry before you leave by feeding them a small meal or leaving a food toy. A satiated dog is more likely to feel content and calm, which can help prevent separation anxiety. However, remember to take your dog's daily food allowance into account to avoid overfeeding.

3. Minimise Disturbances

Some dogs are prone to barking when they see or hear people or other dogs outside. This behaviour can be disruptive and even distressing for both the dog and the owner. Fortunately, there are steps that can be taken to prevent barking and disturbances.

One effective method is to close the curtains or blinds to reduce the amount of visual stimulation that your dog receives from the outside. This can help to decrease their excitement levels and minimize their barking. Another option is to leave your dog in a quiet room away from the windows, with some background noise like the radio or TV turned on to help mask outside sounds.

It's important to note that while these strategies can be helpful, they should not be relied on as a long-term solution. If your dog is barking excessively, it's important to address the underlying cause of the behaviour. This may involve working with a professional dog trainer or behaviourist to help your dog learn to manage their excitement and respond to stimuli in a more appropriate way. With patience and consistency, you can help your dog to overcome their barking tendencies and enjoy a peaceful home environment.

4 Get a Dog Sitter

As a dog owner, it is important to remember that leaving your furry friend alone for extended periods can cause them stress and anxiety. While it's recommended not to leave your dog alone for more than four hours, some dogs may struggle with being alone even for shorter periods.

If you notice that your dog becomes anxious within minutes of you leaving or even before you leave, it's essential to take action to help them feel more comfortable. One option is to hire a dog sitter or dog walking service. Having someone there to keep your dog company and take them for a walk can ease their stress and make them feel more secure.

Additionally, there are other steps you can take to help your dog feel more comfortable when you're not there, such as providing them with plenty of mental stimulation, like puzzle toys or interactive games. You can also leave on some background noise, like a radio or TV, to provide a sense of familiarity and comfort.

Remember, as a responsible dog owner, it's important to prioritize your dog's well-being and ensure that they feel safe and comfortable, even when you're not there.

5.Never Punish Your Dog

It's important to remember that your dog might misbehave while you're out, but showing disapproval when you come back is not the way to handle the situation. Yelling or punishing your dog may cause more anxiety and worsen the behaviour, such as chewing and barking.

When dogs are scolded for their actions, they may exhibit signs of guilt such as lowering their heads, putting their ears back, and tucking their tail between their legs. However, this is not an indication that they know they've done something wrong.

If your dog misbehaves, it's crucial not to react negatively. Bringing your dog to the scene of the mess and expressing anger will only make your dog more anxious and may not even understand the connection between the behaviour and your anger.

Instead, remain calm and take your dog outside while you clean up the mess. It's essential not to physically punish or shout at your dog as this may damage the relationship between you and your furry friend.

Remember, dogs thrive on positive reinforcement, so try to focus on rewarding good behaviour rather than punishing bad behaviour. Positive reinforcement can be something as simple as a treat or a pat on the head.

Top tip: If you do find yourself coming home to a mess, try to avoid even letting your dog see that you're annoyed. Let them outside before cleaning up, and don't react negatively towards them.

Letting Your Dog 'Cry it Out'

It's not uncommon for some dog training guides to recommend the "cry it out" method, where a dog is left alone to cry or bark until they stop. However, this technique can be quite harmful to a dog's overall well-being.

When a dog is left to cry it out, they quickly learn that being alone is a frightening experience. The dog's natural instincts are to be with their pack, or their human family, so being left alone can be a highly stressful and upsetting experience for them.

As the dog becomes more and more distressed, stress hormones like cortisol begin to flood their body. These hormones can take days to reduce and can have negative, long-term effects on the dog's body and mental state. This can lead to increased anxiety and fearfulness, which can then make it even more difficult for the dog to handle being alone in the future.

Furthermore, some dogs may learn that calling for their owner or barking for attention simply doesn't work. They may become resigned to their situation and learn to suffer in silence, which can be detrimental to their emotional well-being.

Rather than resorting to the "cry it out" method, there are other, more humane ways to help your dog cope with being alone. For example, gradually increasing the amount of time your dog spends alone and providing plenty of positive reinforcement can help to reduce their anxiety and make the experience less stressful for them. Additionally, engaging in regular training and exercise can help to build your dog's confidence and reduce their overall anxiety levels.

How To Potty Train If You Work All Day

As a busy individual, it's essential to consider whether getting a puppy is a wise decision. Puppies require a lot of time, attention, and care to develop into well-behaved and healthy dogs. Before making a commitment, it's crucial to evaluate your lifestyle, work schedule, and living situation to determine if you can provide a suitable home for a young dog.

In some cases, adopting an older dog that is already potty trained may be a better option. There are many potty-trained dogs in animal shelters and rescue organizations waiting for a loving home. By adopting an older dog, you can avoid the time-consuming process of potty training a puppy and provide a home for a deserving animal.

However, if you are set on getting a puppy or already have one, potty training is still achievable, but it will require more effort and patience, especially if you work full-time. Here are two solid options to help you.

1. Find a Dog Carer

To make the potty-training process easier, it's crucial to find a qualified caregiver who can help you while you're at work. Consider hiring a professional dog walker or pet sitter who has experience in potty training and caring for young dogs.

Professional dog walkers can take your puppy out for regular potty breaks during the day, keeping them on a consistent routine and reinforcing good habits. Some dog walker services offer individual or group walks, depending on your puppy's socialization needs. In addition to potty breaks, dog walkers can provide exercise and socialization opportunities for your puppy, which are crucial for their physical and mental health.

Pet sitters can also be a great option for busy pet parents. They can come to your home to care for your puppy while you're at work, providing potty breaks, feeding, playtime, and even some basic training. With a pet sitter, your puppy can stay in their familiar surroundings, reducing the stress and anxiety of being in a new environment.

When selecting a dog walker or pet sitter, be sure to do your research and choose a reputable provider. Look for someone with positive reviews and references, and who has experience working with puppies. It's essential to choose someone who you feel comfortable leaving your puppy with and who will provide the best care possible.

If you do need to leave your puppy for long periods of time then here is a method on how to still get them toilet trained around your work schedule

Method

1. The puppy should be taken out to potty first thing in the morning before going to work.
2. Feed him breakfast and then take him out once again before being placed in the crate. When placed in the crate, the pup should be provided with a safe chew toy stuffed with treats to keep him occupied.
3. Have a friend, neighbour, relative, pet walker, or pet sitter swing by twice in the day, first during mid-morning to take the puppy out, then out to potty again before noon.
4. Feed the pup his meal at noon and then take him out again after his meal (and hopefully exercise him again).
5. Stop by again in mid-afternoon for another potty break.

Afternoon to Evening Potty-Break Schedule: When to Take Your Pup Out

- When you first get home
- Before his evening meal
- After his evening meal
- In the middle of the evening
- Right before going to bed
- Once or twice during the night or early morning hours

2. Set a Long Term Confinement Area

Creating a safe, designated area for your puppy to relieve themselves is crucial for successful potty training. Choose a location in your home that is easily accessible and can be designated as the "potty area." This could be a small room, playpen, or gated area that is easy to clean and supervise. Ensure the area is free of hazards or objects that could harm your puppy.

Cover the area with puppy pads or newspaper to protect your floors and make clean-up easier. Puppies are likely to have accidents, so it's essential to accept that potty training may take some time, and accidents may happen. Be patient and consistent in reinforcing positive behaviour while correcting negative behaviour.

It's important to note that using puppy pads or newspaper can create confusion for your puppy, as it's similar to indoor surfaces. As your puppy progresses in potty training, gradually transition them to outdoor potty breaks to reinforce good habits. Additionally, be sure to change the puppy pads or newspaper frequently to maintain a clean and hygienic environment for your puppy.

Remember, successful potty training requires patience, consistency, and positive reinforcement. With a dedicated potty area and a bit of persistence, your puppy will learn to relieve themselves in the appropriate location in due time.

<u>Can You Use a Litter Box for Dogs?</u>

Some puppy owners like using litter boxes. For pups destined to potty outdoors on grass, puppy owners may use litter boxes with fake or real grass so that the pup develops a substrate preference for grass.

Tip: Keep your puppy's food and water in one area and some interactive, safe toys and their bed at the farthest corner away from the potty area. By nature, puppies (other than store-bought puppies or puppy mill dogs) are reluctant to potty near where they eat, play, or sleep.

The use of long-term confinement areas for puppies has both advantages and disadvantages. On the one hand, it can be an effective tool for preventing accidents around the house, especially during the early stages of potty training. By confining the puppy to a specific area, such as an Xpen or a puppy-proofed room, they are more likely to learn to use a designated indoor area to potty. Additionally, long-term confinement areas can provide more room for the puppy to stretch and walk around, allowing them to burn off some energy even when you're not able to supervise them.

On the other hand, there are some disadvantages to using long-term confinement areas, particularly when it comes to potty training. Since the puppy goes potty indoors, they may come to learn that it's acceptable to do so, which can create problems when you try to transition them to outdoor potty breaks. Additionally, because the puppy goes potty when they need to, they won't learn how to "hold it" in the same way that crate training teaches, which can make it more difficult to potty train them in the long run.

Finally, it's important to remember that using a long-term confinement area means you need to rush home right away when your shift is over, as you can't leave your puppy alone for extended periods of time. This can be a disadvantage if you were hoping to have some social time with your co-workers after work or if you have other obligations that require you to be away from home for extended periods of time.

Leaving your Puppy Outside

Another option for potty training a puppy while working is to delegate them to the backyard. However, this can be problematic, as unsupervised puppies may get into trouble, such as ingesting harmful objects, leading to costly vet bills and even surgeries. They may also engage in problematic behaviours like digging, barking, chewing, or trying to escape.

Allowing your puppy to roam in the yard also creates confusion about where to relieve themselves, preventing successful potty training inside the house. Additionally, leaving your puppy alone in the yard puts them at risk of theft, poisoning, teasing, extreme weather conditions, and potential danger from wild animals such as snakes, skunks, raccoons, or birds of prey, or stray dogs

It's essential to consider the potential risks before delegating your puppy to the backyard. Providing a safe and secure environment with appropriate supervision and potty training will lead to a happy, healthy, and well-behaved puppy.

What about Doggie Daycare?

For pet owners who work long hours, finding a safe and engaging environment for their furry friend can be a challenge. Fortunately, doggy daycare has emerged as a popular option, offering a variety of benefits for both pets and owners alike. In this post, we'll explore the benefits of using a doggy daycare and how to choose a good facility.

Benefits of Doggy Daycare for Puppies Socialization: Socialization is vital for puppies to learn good manners and develop healthy relationships with other dogs and humans. Doggy daycare provides a controlled environment where puppies can interact with other dogs and receive positive reinforcement from experienced staff. This helps them become well-adjusted, friendly, and well-behaved adult dogs.

Exercise and Playtime: Puppies are energetic and require plenty of exercise and playtime to burn off their energy. Doggy daycare provides a safe and stimulating environment where puppies can run, jump, and play with other dogs and toys. This not only helps with their physical development but also improves their mental well-being.

Potty Training: Consistent potty training is crucial for puppies to develop good habits. Doggy daycare can provide frequent potty breaks and reinforce positive behaviour, helping puppies learn faster and more effectively.

Reduced Separation Anxiety: Puppies are social animals and can experience separation anxiety when left alone for long periods. Doggy daycare provides a social environment that can reduce anxiety and improve their overall well-being.

How to Choose a Good Doggy Daycare Facility Research: Do your research before choosing a facility. Look for reviews and feedback from other pet owners, and check if the facility has any certifications or awards for pet care.

Facility Standards: A good doggy daycare should have clean and well-maintained facilities with plenty of space for the dogs to play and rest. Check if the facility provides outdoor areas, climate control, and adequate ventilation.

Staff Qualifications: Experienced staff who are passionate about pet care are essential for a good doggy daycare. Ensure that the facility has well-trained staff who can handle emergencies, provide first aid, and understand dog behaviour.

Safety: Safety is crucial in any pet care facility. Look for a daycare that has a secure environment, including fencing, gates, and surveillance cameras.

Conclusion Doggy daycare is an excellent option for pet owners who work long hours and want to provide a safe and engaging environment for their furry friend. It offers numerous benefits, including socialization, exercise, potty training, and reduced anxiety. When choosing a facility, research, facility standards, staff qualifications, and safety should be top considerations to ensure the best possible care for your puppy.

How to Potty Train a Puppy With Pee Pads: 4 Easy Steps

Training your puppy to use pee pads is a practical and convenient option for pet owners who live in apartments or condos without yards, or those who are away from home for extended periods. However, the process can be challenging, and it requires time, patience, and consistency to achieve success.

Here are some tips and steps that you can follow to train your puppy to use pee pads effectively:

1. Choose the Right Pee Pad Choosing the right type of pee pad for your puppy is important. There are many brands and sizes of pee pads available in the market, so select one that is the right size for your puppy and fits your space. It's essential to stick to the same brand of pee pad throughout the training process since changing brands can confuse your puppy.

2. Select a Designated Potty Spot Choose a specific area in your home where your puppy will be allowed to do their business. This area should be easily accessible and visible to your puppy, and should not be too close to their bed or food bowl. By designating a particular spot for potty training, your puppy will learn that this is the only place where they should relieve themselves.

3. Show Your Puppy Where to Go Introduce your puppy to the designated potty spot by bringing them there consistently. Use a leash to lead your puppy to the pee pad area, and give them a command, such as "go potty"

or "do your business," to associate the spot with the act of eliminating waste. Repeat this process every few hours, especially after meals, naps, or playtime, and monitor your puppy's behaviour for signs of needing to go.

4. Praise Your Puppy When your puppy successfully uses the pee pad, offer them lots of praise, affection, and a treat. Positive reinforcement is a powerful tool in training your puppy, and it will help them associate good behaviour with rewards. Avoid punishing your puppy for accidents since it may make them fearful or anxious, and can slow down the training process.

5. Be Consistent Consistency is the key to successfully training your puppy to use pee pads. Stick to a regular feeding and potty schedule, and take your puppy to the designated potty spot every time they need to go. Use the same commands and positive reinforcement techniques every time, and avoid deviating from the routine.

In addition to the above steps, there are a few other materials that may come in handy during potty training. Along with a supply of pee pads, you may find a timer helpful to remind you when to take your puppy to the designated spot. This consistency is so important in reinforcing the potty training that you are giving your puppy. Also, having dog treats on hand will reward your puppy for good behaviour and reinforce the association between using the pad and positive outcomes.

1. Choose a Pee Pad

The first step is to settle on a specific brand of pee pad and choose a size. Some dog owners prefer to try pads that resemble grass. However, those may require additional maintenance. They typically involve a drain system to hold your puppy's pee underneath the plastic grass, which would need to be emptied and cleaned at least once a week

Regular plastic pee pads are an easy choice, but it's important to choose a quality brand, and a good size that you will stick with since changing brands can confuse your puppy. It's best to choose a size that's larger than you need for more coverage.

2. Choose a Potty Spot

Designate a spot where you want your puppy's potty spot to be. Try to choose an area of your home where you can easily keep an eye on your puppy, but the area or room should be somewhat confined.

It's best to avoid carpet as much as possible, for obvious reasons. Also, keep in mind that you should choose somewhere that can serve as a long-term spot for the training pads because moving it around in the future could interfere with training your puppy.

3. Show Your Puppy Where to Go

You should take your puppy to the pad often; a puppy usually cannot hold his bladder for very long. Even an hour is often too long for a puppy. Because the objective is to teach your puppy to go to the pee pad whenever they need to, you may want to use a leash to guide your puppy to the designated spot.

When to Guide Your Puppy to the Pee Pad:

- After eating
- After waking up
- After playing
- Every two hours

Set your timer to go off every two hours. When it goes off, you should walk your puppy over to the pee pad and wait to see what happens. It can be frustrating, and patience is definitely required, but it's important so that your puppy will grow into a fully potty-trained dog.

4. Praise Your Puppy

You can encourage your puppy to go to the bathroom by saying phrases like "go potty," "go pee," etc.

When your puppy actually uses the pad, showing praise is the most effective thing you can do to reinforce this behaviour Tell your puppy that they've been a good boy or good girl, and give him or her a treat or two. However, if you wait several minutes and your puppy doesn't go to the bathroom on the pads, you should wait to try again later. It may be tempting to keep waiting and see what happens, but the process doesn't work that way. Unfortunately, accidents are necessary for the training to be effective.

Be Firm But Don't Scold

Your puppy is bound to have an accident away from the pads, and that's the right opportunity to enforce the idea that it's not where it should go to the bathroom.

You don't need to scold. In fact, aggressive tones and yelling will just scare your puppy. A stern "no" is good, and you should immediately pick up your puppy and take him or her to the pee pad as quickly as possible. It can be especially helpful if you catch your puppy as they're having an accident instead of after.

Proper Cleaning to Prevent More Accidents

One effective way to prevent more accidents is to properly clean the areas where they happen. Have you ever noticed that dogs like to go to the bathroom in the same spot over and over? The reason for this is that dogs are scent driven.

If your dog smells a remaining scent from an old accident, he will be triggered by the scent to go again in the same spot. It is very important that you completely neutralize the scent from any accidents that are not on the pee pads.

Use a pet odor cleaner that is specifically designed to eliminate this odour I have used Nature's Miracle for this task for many years with great results (see below). Nature's miracle has specific enzymes that are designed to break down the scents that dogs pick up on.

My Technique for Erasing an Accident:

1. Pick up the puppy's poop or clean up the urine.
2. After cleaning the area, spray liberally with a stain or odor remover.
3. Let the area sit for about 10 minutes; this will allow time for the enzymes to neutralize the scent.
4. Blot the area dry with a paper towel.

This process, although a little more involved than just cleaning up the accident alone, is well worth your time. It should completely break down the odor, ensuring that your dog doesn't develop a habit of going potty in the same inappropriate spot over and over.

Common Mistakes and Problems

- **Putting Down a Pee Pad Wherever There's an Accident:** This is a bad idea because not only will it confuse your puppy, but the point of pee pad training is that there is one designated spot where your puppy should be going to the bathroom.

- **Punishment for Accidents**: It's very easy to assume that yelling 'bad dog' repeatedly and making a big deal out of their mess will help, but it actually does the opposite. As mentioned before, it will just scare your puppy and will distract from what you're trying to train him or her to do.

- **Troubles Confining Your Puppy to One Area:** Confinement is important because it's easier to potty train a puppy if he or she is limited to one section of your home. Of course, you don't need to keep your puppy confined to one area permanently, but while the training process is going on, it may be a good idea.

If you're having trouble finding a good space to confine your puppy, you could purchase baby gates. It's an easy solution that will keep your puppy where you want him to be. Make sure that the space is within your eyesight, though, so you can monitor your puppy.

Remember: Patience and Consistency Are Key!

These are the basic principles for successfully potty training your new puppy to relieve himself only on pee pads. Although it can be very frustrating and it's tempting to give up at times, it'll be entirely worth it when your puppy is finally trained.

Remember, patience and extreme consistency are the keys to success here. If you start to vary your routine at all (i.e., repeatedly changing the length of time between trips to the pads, changing the brand of pads, or changing the pee pad location), it can and likely will confuse your puppy, setting you back significantly with your potty training.

Being a good pet owner requires responsibility and commitment towards your furry friend. It involves providing your pet with proper nutrition, exercise, shelter, and medical care, as well as socialization and training. As a pet owner, you should also be aware of your pet's needs and behaviour and be able to respond to them accordingly.

Successfully toilet training a new dog can have numerous benefits for both you and your pet. It can prevent unwanted accidents in the house, reduce the risk of behavioural issues, and strengthen the bond between you and your pet. Additionally, it can make your life easier and less stressful as you won't have to constantly clean up after your dog. Overall, effective toilet training is an essential aspect of responsible pet ownership that can lead to a happier, healthier, and more harmonious relationship with your furry friend

Don't miss out!

Visit the website below and you can sign up to receive emails whenever Amanda Walker publishes a new book. There's no charge and no obligation.

https://books2read.com/r/B-A-XDVX-SSSHC

BOOKS 2 READ

Connecting independent readers to independent writers.

Did you love *Toilet Train Your Dog In Seven Days*? Then you should read *Litter Train Your Kitten in 7 Days*[1] by Amanda Walker!

[2]

The Ultimate Guide to a Smooth Transition to Outdoor Toilet Training" is a comprehensive guide that teaches cat owners how to litter train their kittens in just one week, followed by a seamless transition to outdoor toilet training. The book covers everything from selecting the right litter box and litter type to introducing the kitten to the litter box and troubleshooting common issues. The step-by-step approach ensures that both the kitten and the owner are comfortable with the training process.

---

1. https://books2read.com/u/mdX5ZZ

2. https://books2read.com/u/mdX5ZZ

With easy-to-follow instructions and practical tips, this book is the ultimate resource for cat owners looking to achieve a happy and healthy relationship with their feline friends. Keywords: litter training, kitten, toilet training, outdoor, transition, litter box, litter type, training process.

Also by Amanda Walker

Help Me Pay My Bills - Ways To Earn Additional Money
Toilet Train Your Dog In Seven Days
Litter Train Your Kitten in 7 Days
Beyond Binary: Understanding Transgenderism and Gender
Identity in the 21st Century